Prepositions Say "UNDER WHERE?"

by Michael Dahl

illustrated by Maira Chiodi

PICTURE WINDOW BOOKS
a capstone imprint

Prepositions aren't very big words,
but they are very important words.

5

A preposition shows the relationship between a noun (or pronoun) and another word or words in a sentence.

Prepositions add information to a sentence. They help make things clearer.

We would be lost **without** prepositions!

No more hot pretzels **with** mustard! Or tacos **with** cheese!

From: Shirley To: Michael

Prepositions of place tell where something is.

Prepositions of movement show how people and objects move from one place to another.

How will I ever find my little phone **in** this big city?

MAPS HERE

This map will help! See, the water flows **from** here **to** there. So we go **across** town, **around** the shopping mall, then **into** the sewer system, **through** this long tunnel, **up** the pipes, **along** the gloopy pools, **down** the stairs, **toward** the waterfall, **onto** the bridge, and finally **past** the junkyard.

Is that all? Easy-peasy! Let's go!

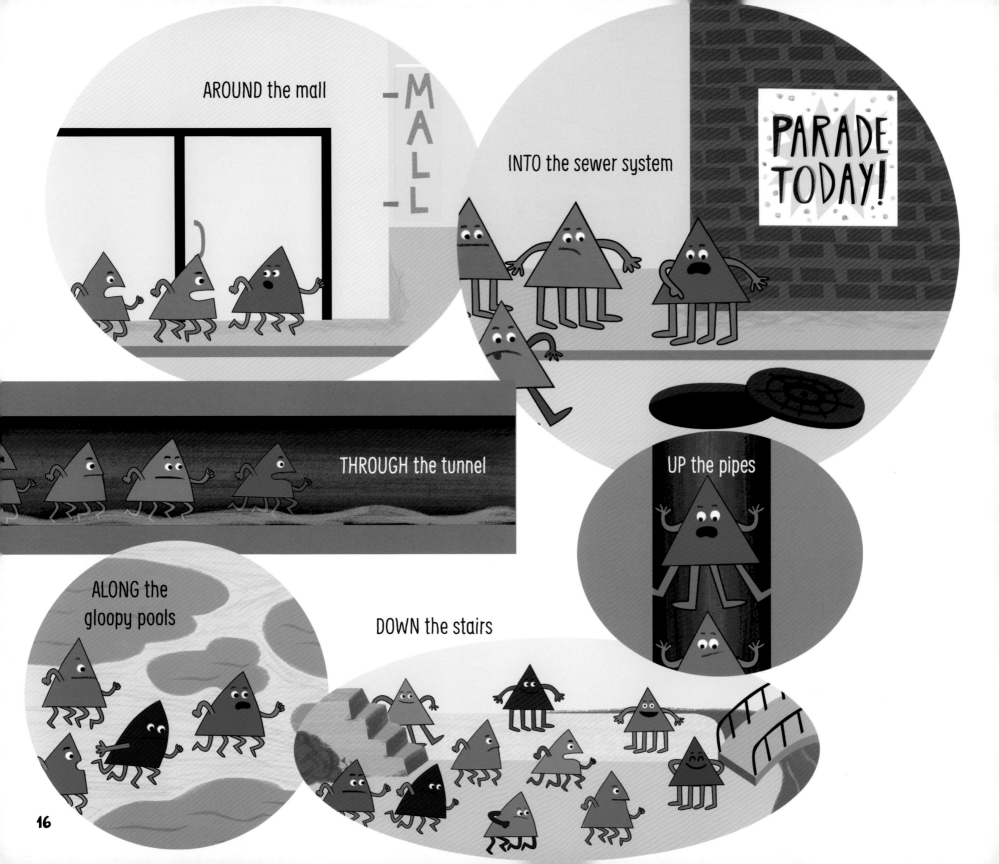

Prepositions are good leaders. They are always the first word in a prepositional phrase.

Wow, it floated **beneath** the entire city!

preposition   modifier object

prepositional phrase

I see the phone! It's **in** the stream!

preposition   object

prepositional phrase

We need to reread the text about what to do **before** the parade, **during** the parade, and **after** the parade.

Good thing the phone was **inside** a waterproof case that floats!

Parade? Oh no! We forgot **about** the parade!

Prepositions of time tell when things happen.

Got it!
Sorry. We don't want to tell you how to do your job. But we're prepositions! We know how to get anywhere!

22

25

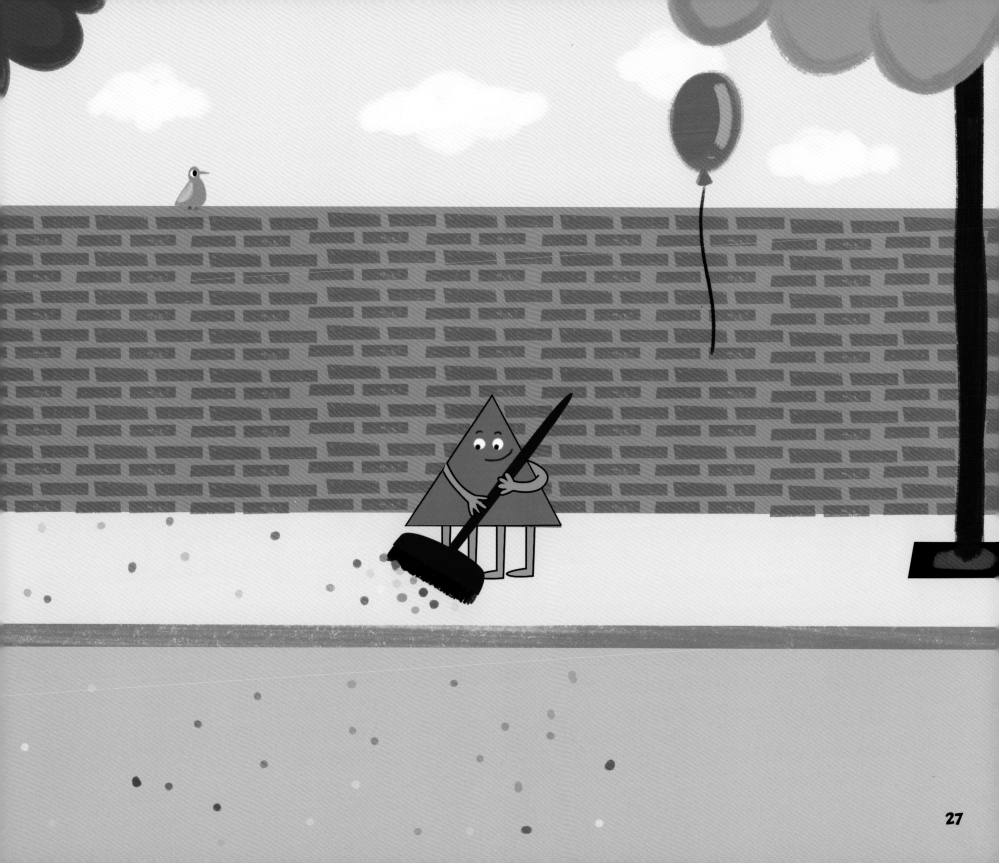

PREPOSITIONS ON PARADE

Prepositions show relationships between nouns (or pronouns) and other words in a sentence.

Starfish live UNDER the sea. ("Starfish" and "sea" are nouns. "Under" is the preposition that tells us where the starfish are in relation to the sea.)
The starfish are crawling ON the rocks. (Where are the starfish in relation to the rocks?)
Hold the starfish carefully IN your hand. (Where are the starfish in relation to your hand?)

Some prepositions tell us when things happen.

The bulldog snored FOR an hour.
Band practice starts AT one o'clock.

Prepositions show us where people and things move in the world.

The goats run AROUND the tree.
The motorcycle zooms PAST the bicycle.
Please carry the groceries UP the stairs.
I like walking THROUGH the bookstore.

Prepositional phrases are groups of words that start with a preposition and contain an object and any words that modify the object.

AFTER the long, exciting race
IN my purple pajamas

Once you have flipped THROUGH all the pages OF this book, you may set it ON the shelf, lay it ON a table, or put it NEXT to you and make a list OF all the prepositions you can find AROUND you.

ABOUT THE AUTHOR

Michael Dahl is the author of more than 200 books for children and has won the AEP Distinguished Achievement Award three times for his nonfiction. He is the author of the bestselling *Bedtime for Batman* and *You're a Star, Wonder Woman!* picture books. He has written dozens of books of jokes, riddles, and puns. He likes to play with words. In grade school, he read the dictionary for fun. Really. Michael is proud to say that he has always been a noun. A PROPER noun, at that.

ABOUT THE ILLUSTRATOR

Maira Chiodi's colorful, joyful work has appeared in magazines, books, games, and a variety of other products. As a child in Brazil, Maira spent hours cutting paper, painting, and reading—creating wildly imaginative worlds all her own. Today she feels lucky to be able to create and share her illustrations and designs with kids and grown-ups around the world. She divides her time between Canada and Brazil, finding inspiration for her art in nature, animation, and the culture of her native country.

GLOSSARY

modify—to change or provide further detail about something; words that do this are called modifiers

noun—a word that names a person, place, or thing

preposition—a word that shows the relationship between a noun (or pronoun) and another word or words in a sentence

prepositional phrase—a group of words that expresses a thought, starts with a preposition, and contains an object and any words that modify the object

pronoun—a word that takes the place of a noun

THINK ABOUT IT

1. Think about the path you take from your home to school. How would you give someone directions by using prepositions of movement? Turn to page 15 for help.

2. Make a list of eight items in your classroom. Then describe where they are by using the prepositions of place shown on pages 12 and 13. For example, "Our class turtle is INSIDE his tank."

READ MORE

Doyle, Sheri. *What Is a Preposition? Parts of Speech.* North Mankato, MN: Capstone Press, 2013.

Ganeri, Anita. *Describing Words: Adjectives, Adverbs, and Prepositions. Getting to Grips with Grammar.* Chicago: Heinemann Library, 2012.

Walton, Rick. *Around the House, the Fox Chased the Mouse: An Adventure in Prepositions.* Layton, UT: Gibbs Smith, 2011.

INTERNET SITES

Enchanted Learning: Grammar: Preposition
https://www.enchantedlearning.com/grammar/
partsofspeech/prepositions/index.shtml

Grammaropolis: The Prepositions
https://www.grammaropolis.com/preposition.php

Schoolhouse Rock: Prepositions
https://www.youtube.com/watch?v=yfExXGMX2JM

LOOK FOR ALL THE PARTS OF SPEECH TITLES

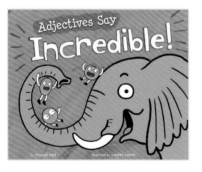

31

INDEX

Editor: Jill Kalz
Designer: Lori Bye
Production Specialist: Katy LaVigne
The illustrations in this book were created digitally.

Picture Window Books are published by Capstone
1710 Roe Crest Drive, North Mankato, Minnesota 56003
www.capstonepub.com

Library of Congress Cataloging-in-Publication Data
Names: Dahl, Michael, author.
Title: Prepositions say "under where?" / by Michael Dahl.
Description: 1st edition. | North Mankato, Minnesota : Picture Window Books, [2020] |
Series: Nonfiction picture books. Word adventures : parts of speech
Identifiers: LCCN 2019004147| ISBN 9781515840985 (library binding) |
ISBN 9781515841067 (paperback) | ISBN 9781515841029 (eBook PDF)
Subjects: LCSH: English language—Prepositions—Juvenile literature. |
English language—Grammar—Juvenile literature.
Classification: LCC PE1335 .D34 2020 | DDC 428.2—dc23
LC record available at https://lccn.loc.gov/2019004147

All internet sites appearing in back matter were available and accurate when this book was sent to press.

Printed and bound in China.
001654